This is a story of a boy in a
real castle nearly eight hundred years ago

Will lived in a castle.
He was a spit boy.
He stood by the fire and cooked the meat.

1

"Take this food to the soldiers on
the wall," said the cook, "and be
quick about it!"
Will was glad to get away from the hot fire.

Will liked going up onto the castle walls.
You could see for miles up there.
But today the soldiers looked worried.
"What's the matter?" asked Will.

"Look over there, boy," said one of
the soldiers.
"That's the Grey Fox and his men.
The Grey Fox wants to steal
this castle from Lord Robert."

"I wish I was a knight," said Will to himself.
"I would drive away the Grey Fox!"
"Will! Will!" cried the cook.
"The spit needs turning."

5

Will was kept busy all day.
He took food to the Great Hall.
There was no music or dancing today.
Lord Robert and his knights were
wearing their armour.

Will took food to John the blacksmith, who
was working very hard.
"Is the Grey Fox going to
attack the castle?" asked Will.

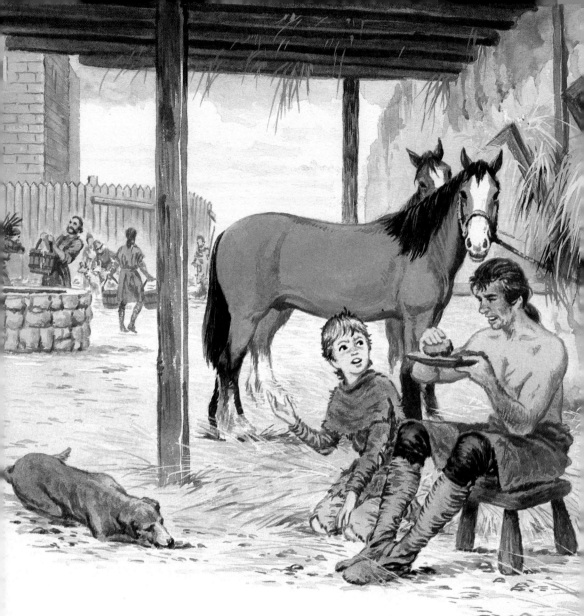

"I think so, Will," said John.
"But don't worry.
It's a strong castle, and we have
plenty of food and water.
He won't make us give in."

It was very late when Will got to bed.
He slept in the stables.
He liked the horses, and there was
plenty of hay for his bed.

Will was soon asleep, but not for long.
Something woke him up.
It was the noise of someone digging.
But who could be digging in the
middle of the night?

Will called John the blacksmith.
"It's the Grey Fox!" said John.
"His men are trying to dig a hole under
the wall to get into the castle!"

As soon as it was light, Lord Robert sent
his soldiers out of the castle gates.
His soldiers drove the
enemy away from the wall.

Suddenly a huge stone hit the castle walls.
Arrows fell from the sky.
"Attack!" shouted the Grey Fox.
"Break down the castle gates!"

His men tried to break down the gates.
But the gates were too strong.
They tried to climb over the castle walls.
But the walls were too high.

At last the fighting stopped.
The Grey Fox and his men crept away.
"Well done, boy!" said John.
"You stopped them from digging under
the walls!"

Will felt like a hero.
He told all the other children about
how clever he was.
Then someone grabbed him by the ear.
"Time to get back to your spit," said the cook.